The First Seahorse

A Story of the *Star Horses*

Illustrated by
Jenna Leigh

Lauren Marie

For Grandma Lulu and Papa Bill

Horses gallop through the stars up high,
Tied to the elements of the magical sky.
First of them all is the Lord of the Sun,
Blazing as he continues his celestial run.

The Lord's first son was the Prince of Starlight,
A shimmering white horse who gleamed in the night.
Eternally he sought for power and fame;
To be Lord of All was his foremost aim.

The Princess of the Moon was the lunar mare,
A fair golden horse with moonlit hair.
She ruled the moon as it waxed and waned;
The winds and the tides were in Luna's domain.

Twice a day, she made tides rise and fall,
Astride the moon as she oversaw it all—
Fine sailing vessels with carved wooden prows,
And dolphin pods riding the waves from their bows.

Luna's dearest ship was the Lady Louan,
Who sailed from Plymouth to the Sea of Japan.
Captain Bill was her intrepid skipper;
He traveled the world with his belovéd clipper.

They traded in spices, fine silks and teas,
Voyaging across the seven blue seas,
Helped by Luna, who watched from above,
Giving steady tides as a show of her love.

The Prince grew angry when he saw her affection;
He thought the moon should be under his direction.
"You can't have a favorite; it isn't fair,"
He called out his challenge to the lunar mare.

"I deserve the moon's power more than you;
The time has come for me to start my coup."
He snorted and reared to his magnificent height,
Shining with power and brilliant white light.

Luna stamped a hoof and bugled defiantly back,
Her foot coming down with a moon-shaking crack.
"You cannot win, the moon is rightfully mine;
I am the master of its power divine."

Luna stood her ground, muscles all tensed,
Then the Prince struck out, and the battle commenced.
Luna snapped and kicked, reared and wheeled,
Determined to force her rival to yield.

But the Prince fought back and matched every strike;
Neither gained an edge, they were too much alike.
The Prince cried, "Surrender, and I'll let you go."
"Never!" she neighed, then lunged at her foe.

The battle raged on for control of the moon,
Creating on Earth a tremendous typhoon.
Bill reefed the sails as the storm began,
Preparing to endure it with the Lady Louan.

Around the ship, the waves rose higher and higher;
There had never been a storm more dire.
Lightning flashed bright, and thunder boomed loud,
And rain poured down from the roiling clouds.

A great wave arose, smashing into the ship,
And with a groan of timber, she began to flip.
The sailors cried out as they fell from the deck,
Certain they'd perish in the stormy shipwreck.

Luna saw their peril and abandoned the fight,
Determined to save them from their treacherous plight.
The Prince trumpeted his victory across the skies,
And returned to the moon, his hard-won prize.

Luna raced toward the Earth and the floundering ship;
The sailors were caught in the sea's merciless grip,
Treading the water and fighting huge waves—
They'd never encountered a situation so grave.

Luna plunged into the heaving gray sea,
But was quickly confronted with reality:
She was a horse, with hooves and not fins,
And in the wild waters, she could barely swim.

A flash of lightning allowed Bill to spot her,
As they both kicked furiously in the frigid saltwater.
"Please help us," he cried, "for only you can.
Save the crew of the Lady Louan!"

There was one last thing that Luna could do—
She had to become something brand-new:
A horse of the sea, not of the moon.
Only then could she beat the terrible typhoon.

Luna gathered her strength and made her decision;
She focused her mind on force and precision.
Her body began to morph and change,
Becoming a creature both new and strange.

Luna became the first-ever seahorse,
Her life now set on an uncharted course.
But as she swam to the rescue, she found a big flaw—
She was minuscule now, she suddenly saw.

But being tied to the ocean gave her a new feature:
She could now speak with every sea creature.
A pod of dolphins caught her eye,
And she called out for help as they swam by.

"Why should we help?" they asked with a grin.
"Perhaps men shouldn't sail if they cannot swim."
Luna replied, "These are the sailors that I cherish,
Please help me now, or they will certainly perish."

The dolphins debated, then said, "Sounds fun!
We have the means to get the job done."
With a flip of their tails, and a turn of their flippers,
They picked up and rescued the crew of the clipper.

As they headed toward land, Luna swam alongside,
Her tiny new body bursting with pride.
The pod dropped their riders near a sandy beach,
Safely beyond the storm's deadly reach.

Joy filled Luna as the sailors called thanks;
She had found a new home in the dolphin pod's ranks.
And the ocean's power was under her decree,
For she had become the Queen of the Sea.

From that day forth, dolphins had a new vocation,
And they became known as heroic cetaceans.
They saved shipwrecked sailors with their gallant acts,
Carrying them to safety on their broad gray backs.

Captain Bill set sail on the fair Lady Lulu,
A brand-new ship with his faithful old crew.
The Prince watched the Earth from the moon up above,
While Luna swam near the sailors she loved.

978-1-949290-45-5 paperback

Cover Art
by
Jenna Leigh

Cover Design
by

A Dragonfeather Book

Dragonfeather Books
a division of
Bedazzled Ink Publishing Company
Fairfield, California
http://www.bedazzledink.com

Lauren Marie has always seen the magic in everyday life. From dragons swooping through the clouds to horses galloping among the stars, magical creatures and majestic nature have always been intertwined in Lauren's imagination. Lauren lives in Northern California with Star Horses of her own.

Jenna Leigh was born and raised in Southern California. Her childhood passion for drawing, sketching, and painting horses matured into her realization that she wanted to become a professional artist. She moved to Colorado and earned her Bachelor of Fine Arts degree with an emphasis in painting from Western State Colorado University. Jenna has spent her time as a freelance artist and framer, illustrating works. Her art has won multiple awards, publications in local magazines and newspapers. She specializes in oil, watercolor, and acrylic paintings, and her work has been displayed in multiple galleries and exhibitions.

CPSIA information can be obtained at www.ICGtesting.com
Printed in the USA
LVIW011859060121
675847LV00013BA/132